Inquiry Journal

Level 5

Teacher's Annotated Edition

A Division of The McGraw·Hill Companies

Columbus, Ohio

www.sra4kids.com

SRA/McGraw-Hill

A Division of The McGraw·Hill Companies

Send all inquiries to:
SRA/McGraw-Hill
8787 Orion Place
Columbus, OH 43240-4027

Printed in the United States of America.

ISBN 0-07-569573-1
  2 3 4 5 6 7 8 9 QPD 07 06 05 04 03 02

Table of Contents

Unit 1　Cooperation and Competition

Unit 2　Astronomy

Unit 3　Heritage

Knowledge about Cooperation and Competition

- This is what I know about cooperation and competition before reading the unit.

  Answers will vary.

  _____

  _____

  _____

  _____

  _____

- These are some things about cooperation and competition that I would like to talk about and understand better.

  Answers will vary.

  _____

  _____

  _____

  _____

  _____

  Reminder: I should read this page again when I get to the end of the unit to see how much my ideas about cooperation and competition have changed.

UNIT 1 Cooperation and Competition

Recording Concept Information

As I read each selection, this is what I added to my understanding of cooperation and competition.

- "Class President" by Johanna Hurwitz
  Answers will vary.

  _____

  _____

  _____

  _____

- "The Marble Champ" by Gary Soto
  Answers will vary.

  _____

  _____

  _____

  _____

- "Juggling" by Donna Gamache
  Answers will vary.

  _____

  _____

  _____

  _____

- "The Abacus Contest" by Priscilla Wu
  Answers will vary.

  _____

  _____

  _____

  _____

  _____

- "S.O.R. Losers" by Avi
  Answers will vary.

  _____

  _____

  _____

  _____

  _____

- "Founders of the Children's Rain Forest" by Phillip Hoose
  Answers will vary.

  _____

  _____

  _____

  _____

  _____

UNIT 1   Cooperation and Competition

Charting Examples

As you read and investigate, you will discover many examples of cooperation and competition. Record acts from stories, newspapers, television shows, and your life in the chart below. You can check this chart periodically for investigation ideas and topics.

Answers will vary.

Acts of Cooperation	Acts of Competition

Ideas about Cooperation and Competition

Of the ideas discussed in class about cooperation and competition, these are the ones I found most interesting.

Answers will vary.

_____

_____

_____

_____

_____

_____

_____

_____

_____

_____

_____

_____

_____

_____

_____

_____

Name _____ Date _____

Charting Interview Information

When you have completed your interviews on the positive and negative effects of cooperation and competition, place your findings in the following charts. In the left column of each chart, list whether the situation or event you will describe in the right column had a positive or negative effect.

Answers will vary.

Cooperation	
Effect: Positive or Negative?	**Situation or Event**

Competition	
Effect: Positive or Negative?	**Situation or Event**

Name _____ Date _____

Formulating Questions and Problems

A good question or problem to investigate:
Answers will vary.

_____

_____

_____

_____

_____

Why this is an interesting question or problem:
Answers will vary.

_____

_____

_____

_____

_____

Some other things I wonder about this question or problem:
Answers will vary.

_____

_____

_____

_____

_____

Formulating Questions and Problems *(continued)*

My investigation group's question or problem:

Answers will vary.

_____

_____

_____ .

_____

_____

What our investigation will contribute to the rest of the class:

Answers will vary.

_____

_____

_____

_____

_____

Some other things I wonder about this question or problem:

Answers will vary.

_____

_____

_____

_____

_____

Planning an Interview

Reporters and other writers often interview other people to find out more about their knowledge and experiences. Read the interviewing tips listed below.

- Always ask permission to interview the person. Tell him or her the reason for the interview and how much time you think you will need.
- Decide ahead of time what you want to know.
- Write your questions in an organized order, with space after each one for taking notes.
- Speak clearly, listen carefully, and be polite.
- Take notes as answers are given.
- Thank the person you interviewed for his or her time.
- Read your notes immediately after you leave the interview, while it is still fresh in your mind.

List some people you know who have had experience with cooperation or competition. Has anyone on the list, such as an athlete who plays a team sport, had interesting experiences with both competition and cooperation? Which people do you think would agree to talk with you?

People I might interview:

Answers will vary.

_____

_____

_____

_____

_____

_____

_____

_____

Planning an Interview *(continued)*

Continue to plan your interview by identifying the topics you want to discuss. Then think of three questions you might ask about each topic and write them on the lines provided.

Answers will vary.

Topic to Discuss: _____

_____

Question: _____

_____

Question: _____

_____

Question: _____

_____

Topic to Discuss: _____

_____

Question: _____

_____

Question: _____

_____

Question: _____

_____

Topic to Discuss: _____

_____

Question: _____

_____

Question: _____

_____

Question: _____

_____

Time Management

Often large tasks can be accomplished by one person, but two or three people can finish the task much quicker. In the chart below, list in the first column several large tasks that you do at home or at school. In the second column, list the approximate time it takes you to complete each task by yourself. In the third column, list the approximate time the task would take if you had help. In the last column, calculate the amount of time you would save on each task if you had help.

Answers will vary.

Task	Time Alone	Time with Help	Saved Time

Time Management *(continued)*

Review the chart on the previous page, and record below the amount of time you would save if you had help with your tasks. Then, on the lines provided, write a paragraph about how you would spend the time that you saved. Include details about when you would use the time and where you would spend it. **Answers will vary.**

Total Time Saved: _____

How I Would Spend My Time: _____

_____

_____

_____

_____

_____

_____

_____

_____

_____

_____

_____

_____

_____

_____

Name _____ Date _____

Making Conjectures

Our question or problem:
Answers will vary.

_____

_____

_____

_____

_____

Conjecture (my first theory or explanation):
Answers will vary.

_____

_____

_____

_____

_____

_____

_____

_____

_____

   As you collect information, your conjecture will change.
Return to this page to record your new theories or
explanations about your question or problem.

Name _____ Date _____

Taking Notes

Sports magazines and other periodicals feature stories about popular athletes and major sporting events. At your school or local library, choose a magazine article about an interesting sports figure or competition. On the lines below, take notes about the main points of the article, including some direct quotations, if possible.

Answers will vary.

_____

_____

_____

_____

_____

_____

_____

_____

_____

_____

_____

_____

_____

_____

_____

Organize your notes from the previous page in outline form.

Answers will vary.

Subject: _____

I. _____

    A. _____

    B. _____

    C. _____

II. _____

    A. _____

    B. _____

    C. _____

III. _____

    A. _____

    B. _____

    C. _____

IV. _____

    A. _____

    B. _____

    C. _____

Name _____ Date _____

Project Planning

Use the calendar to help schedule your cooperation and competition unit investigation. Fill in the dates. Make sure that you mark any days you know you will not be able to work. Then choose the date on which you will start and the date on

Sunday	Monday	Tuesday	Wednesday

Project Planning • Inquiry Journal

which you hope to finish. You may also find it helpful to mark the dates by which you hope to complete different parts of the investigation. Record what you accomplish each day.

Answers will vary.

Thursday	Friday	Saturday

UNIT I Cooperation and Competition

Establishing Investigation Needs

My group's question or problem:
Answers will vary.

_____

_____

_____

_____

Knowledge Needs—Information I need to find or figure out
in order to investigate the question or problem: **Answers will vary.**

A. _____

B. _____

C. _____

D. _____

E. _____

Source	Useful?	How?
Encyclopedias		
Books		
Magazines		
Newspapers		
Videotapes, filmstrips, and so on		
Television		
Interviews, observations		
Museums		
Other:		

Name _____ Date _____

Organizing Information

As you continue to investigate the theme of cooperation and competition, it will be helpful to have a system for organizing the information you find. Use the chart below to record sources you are using in your investigation and brief notes on the type of information obtained from each source.

Answers will vary.

Cooperation and Competition	
Sources	**Type of Information**

Name _____ Date _____

UNIT 1 Cooperation and Competition

Winning or Losing Poll

Poll several of your classmates on their feelings about winning, losing, and competition. You can record your information in the chart below. Then organize your poll information on the next page. **Answers will vary.**

Gender	Age	What is more important, winning or enjoying the game? Why?	Do you need a good attitude to win? Why?	Is it important to be good at everything you try to do? Why or why not?

After you have finished polling classmates, write three things you learned from the poll about your classmates' feelings on winning and losing. For example, you might find that girls thought winning was more important than boys did. Note your findings in the space below. **Answers will vary.**

1. _____

_____

_____

_____

_____

2. _____

_____

_____

_____

_____

3. _____

_____

_____

_____

_____

UNIT I Cooperation and Competition

Establishing Investigation Plans

Our question or problem:
Answers will vary.

_____

_____

_____

_____

Knowledge Needs—Information we need to find or figure
out in order to investigate the question or problem:

Answers will vary.

A. _____

B. _____

C. _____

D. _____

E. _____

F. _____

Group Members	Main Jobs

Hint: To save rewriting Knowledge Needs in the
Main Jobs section, put in the capital letter marking
the Knowledge Needs line.

Making a Bibliography

Make a separate note or card for each book in which you have found information for your investigation project. Include the following:

- Author's name—last name first, followed by a comma, then first and middle names or initials—followed by a period.
- Title of the book—underlined or italicized, followed by a period.
- Publisher's name—followed by a comma.
- Date of publication—followed by a period.

Example: Richmond, Robert W. *Kansas: A Land of Contrasts*. Forum Press, 1974.

Use the lines provided to make bibliography entries for three sources you have used for your investigation project. **Answers will vary.**

Source 1: _____

_____

_____

Source 2: _____

_____

_____

Source 3: _____

_____

_____

Note: When creating the bibliography for your investigation project, write or type all of your entries on one document. The entries should appear in alphabetic order by the author's last name.

UNIT 1 Cooperation and Competition

Finding a Cause

The first step in working as a class to support a cause is to find a cause in which all of you are interested. In the first column, write any causes that are of personal interest to you. (For example, your cause may be finding families for homeless pets.) In the second column, list the names of any organizations that support the causes. (For example, an organization that helps place pets in homes is the Humane Society.) Then, in the third column, write the reasons you think each cause is important. When you have completed the chart, compare and discuss your charts with your classmates. Then, as a class, decide which cause or organization to support. **Answers will vary.**

Causes	Organizations	Reasons

After you have decided with the class which cause or organization to support, choose a fundraiser that you would like to host. Write the name of the fundraiser in the first box. Then, list the pros (strengths or good points) and cons (weaknesses or bad points) of the fundraiser you chose. When you have finished, share your chart with others in the class. Then, as a class, you can decide the kind of fundraiser to host and begin planning. **Answers will vary.**

Fundraiser:	
Pros	Cons

Name _____ Date _____

Reading and Using Visual Aids

The following visual aid is called a *pie chart*. Pie charts are used to visually represent percentages, or parts of a whole. Read the pie chart and answer the following questions.

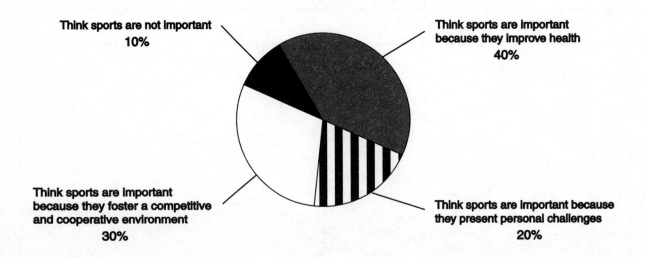

Opinions About Competitive Sports

Think sports are not important
10%

Think sports are important because they improve health
40%

Think sports are important because they foster a competitive and cooperative environment
30%

Think sports are important because they present personal challenges
20%

1. What is the reason most people think sports are important?

   Most people think sports are important because they improve health.

2. What percentage of people polled think sports are not important?

   Ten percent of people polled think sports are not important.

3. What is the second most popular reason for sports being important?

   The second most popular reason is sports foster a competitive and cooperative environment.

4. What percentage of people polled think sports present personal challenges?

 Twenty percent of people polled think sports

 present personal challenges.

5. Can you think of any other reasons sports are important?

 Answers will vary.

_____

   Choose an aspect of cooperation and competition to represent with the use of a visual aid. You might diagram the steps to building a cooperative environment, or you might present a table of sources and topics related to cooperation and competition. Draw your visual aid below.

Name _____ Date _____

Unit Wrap-Up

- How did you feel about this unit?

  ☐ I enjoyed it very much.   ☐ I liked it.

  ☐ I liked some of it.   ☐ I didn't like it.

- How would you rate the difficulty of this unit?

  ☐ easy   ☐ medium   ☐ hard

- How would you rate your performance during this unit?

  ☐ I learned a lot about cooperation and competition.

  ☐ I learned some new things about cooperation and competition.

  ☐ I didn't learn much about cooperation and competition.

- Why did you choose this rating?

  Answers will vary.
  _____

  _____

- What was the most interesting thing you learned about cooperation and competition?

  Answers will vary.
  _____

  _____

- Is there anything else about cooperation and competition that you would like to learn? What?

  Answers will vary.
  _____

  _____

- What did you learn about cooperation and competition that you didn't know before?

  Answers will vary.

- What did you learn about yourself as a learner?

  Answers will vary.

- As a learner, what do you need to work on?

  Answers will vary.

- What resources (books, films, magazines, interviews, other) did you use on your own during this unit? Which of these were the most helpful? Why?

  Answers will vary.

Name _____ Date _____

Knowledge about Astronomy

- This is what I know about astronomy before reading the unit.

    Answers will vary.

    _____

    _____

    _____

    _____

    _____

    _____

    _____

- These are some things I would like to know about astronomy.

    Answers will vary.

    _____

    _____

    _____

    _____

    _____

    _____

Reminder: I should read this page again when I get to the end of the unit to see how much I've learned about astronomy.

Name _____ Date _____

Recording Concept Information

As I read each selection, I learned these new things about astronomy.

- "Galileo" by Navin Sullivan
  Answers will vary.
  _____
  _____
  _____
  _____

- "Telescopes" by David Macaulay
  Answers will vary.
  _____
  _____
  _____
  _____

- "The Heavenly Zoo" by Alison Lurie
  Answers will vary.
  _____
  _____
  _____
  _____

- "Circles, Squares, and Daggers: How Native Americans Watched the Skies" by Elsa Marston

Answers will vary.

_____

_____

_____

_____

_____

_____

_____

_____

_____

- "The Mystery of Mars" by Sally Ride and Tam O'Shaughnessy

Answers will vary.

_____

_____

_____

_____

_____

_____

_____

_____

_____

_____

- "Stars" by Seymour Simon
  Answers will vary.

  _____

  _____

  _____

  _____

  _____

  _____

  _____

  _____

- "The Book That Saved the Earth" by Claire Boiko
  Answers will vary.

  _____

  _____

  _____

  _____

  _____

  _____

  _____

  _____

  _____

Ideas about Astronomy

Of the ideas discussed in class about astronomy, these are the ones I found most interesting.   **Answers will vary.**

_____

_____

_____

_____

_____

_____

_____

_____

_____

_____

_____

_____

_____

_____

_____

_____

_____

_____

Organizing Information in a Chart

The following paragraph contains a great deal of information about the solar system. Make the information easier to follow by organizing it into a chart.

Nine planets revolve around the sun. Mercury is about 35 million miles away from the sun, and Venus is about 67 million miles away. Earth is the third planet, at about 92 million miles away. After Earth comes Mars at 140 million miles, Jupiter at 480 million, Saturn at 880 million, Uranus at 1,800 million, Neptune at 2,800 million, and Pluto at 3,700 million. It takes the planets the following amount of time to orbit the sun: Mercury, 88 days; Venus, 225 days; Earth, 365 days; Mars, 687 days; Jupiter, 11.9 years; Saturn, 29.5 years; Uranus, 84 years; Neptune, 165 years; Pluto, 248 years.

Planet	Distance from Sun in Millions of Miles	Orbit Time
Mercury	35 million	88 days
Venus	67 million	225 days
Earth	92 million	365 days
Mars	140 million	687 days
Jupiter	480 million	11.9 years
Saturn	880 million	29.5 years
Uranus	1,800 million	84 years
Neptune	2,800 million	165 years
Pluto	3,700 million	248 years

Now, give this chart a title that tells what the chart is about:

_____

Organizing Information in a Chart *(continued)*

Now use the following chart to organize the questions and problems you and your classmates have presented during investigation discussions. **Answers will vary.**

Interesting Idea	Who Said It	My Thoughts About the Question

Formulating Questions and Problems

A good question or problem to investigate:
Answers will vary.

_____

_____

_____

_____

_____

Why this is an interesting question or problem:
Answers will vary.

_____

_____

_____

_____

_____

Some other things I wonder about this question or problem:
Answers will vary.

_____

_____

_____

_____

_____

Formulating Questions and Problems *(continued)*

My investigation group's question or problem:
Answers will vary.

What our investigation will contribute to the rest of the class:
Answers will vary.

Some other things I wonder about this question or problem:
Answers will vary.

Making a Diagram

Use the Internet, books, or magazines to investigate what happens during a solar or lunar eclipse. Draw a diagram of a solar lunar eclipse and label the parts.

Write a short description of your diagram.

Diagrams and descriptions will vary, but they should communicate either that a solar eclipse happens when the moon passes between the sun and the earth or that a lunar eclipse happens when the earth passes between the sun and the moon.

UNIT 2 Astronomy

Making Conjectures

Our question or problem:
Answers will vary.

_____

_____

_____

_____

_____

_____

Conjecture (my first theory or explanation):
Answers will vary.

_____

_____

_____

_____

_____

_____

_____

_____

_____

As you collect information, your conjecture will change.
Return to this page to record your new theories or
explanations about your question or problem.

Name _____ Date _____

Using the Card Catalog

```
J          CONSTELLATIONS
QB
802.R47    Rey, H. A.
           Find the Constellations
           written and illustrated by H. A. Rey.
           —Boston, MA: Houghton Mifflin, 1992.
           72 pp.: col. ill.
           Summary: A method for recognizing
           the stars and finding constellations is
           described.
```

Above is an example of a subject card. Copy information from a subject card you have found for a book about stars in the space below.

Answers will vary.

UNIT 2 Astronomy

Project Planning

Use the calendar to help schedule your astronomy unit investigation. Fill in the dates. Make sure that you mark any days you know you will not be able to work. Then choose the date on which you will start and the date on which you hope to

Sunday	Monday	Tuesday	Wednesday

finish. You may also find it helpful to mark the dates by which
you hope to complete different parts of the investigation.
Record what you accomplish each day. **Answers will vary.**

Thursday	Friday	Saturday

Name _____ Date _____

Establishing Investigation Needs

My group's question or problem:
Answers will vary.

_____

_____

_____

_____

_____

Knowledge Needs—Information I need to find or figure out
in order to investigate the question or problem: **Answers will vary.**

A. _____

B. _____

C. _____

D. _____

E. _____

Source	Useful?	How?
Encyclopedias		
Books		
Magazines		
Newspapers		
Videotapes, filmstrips, and so on		
Television		
Interviews, observations		
Museums		
Other:		

Outlining

Use the following outline format to organize knowledge and
sources you need for your investigation.   **Answers will vary.**

I. Question or Problem: _____

_____

   A. Conjecture: _____

       _____

      1. Knowledge needed to prove/disprove conjecture

        a. _____

         _____

        b. _____

         _____

        c. _____

         _____

      2. Sources to investigate

        a. _____

         _____

        b. _____

         _____

        c. _____

         _____

Name _____ Date _____

Establishing Investigation Plans

Our question or problem:
Answers will vary.

_____

_____

_____

_____

Knowledge Needs—Information we need to find or figure
out in order to investigate the question or problem:
Answers will vary.

A. _____

B. _____

C. _____

D. _____

E. _____

F. _____

Group Members	Main Jobs

Hint: To save rewriting Knowledge Needs in the
Main Jobs section, put in the capital letter marking
the Knowledge Needs line.

Using an Index

Use an index of your choice to find information on your group's investigation problem. You may use an index found in the back of a book about your investigation topic or the kind of index that lists titles and authors of publications about astronomy. **Answers will vary.**

A key word, or word related to the topic I am investigating, that I found in the index:

_____

Information I found listed with the key word:

Page numbers: _____

_____

Titles and authors: _____

_____

_____

_____

Other key words that were cross-referenced: _____

_____

_____

Any other information provided: _____

_____

Title and author of the index I used:

_____

_____

_____

UNIT 2 Astronomy

Feedback

   If you gave an informal presentation of your investigation findings, record notes on the feedback you received on the lines provided. Reference these notes as you make decisions about how to revise your presentation. **Answers will vary.**

_____

_____

_____

_____

_____

_____

_____

_____

_____

_____

_____

_____

_____

_____

_____

Using Note Cards

People who give speeches and make presentations often organize their information on note cards. Use the cards below and on the next page to make notes that you could refer to during an oral presentation of your investigation findings.

Answers will vary.

Name _____ Date _____

Self-Evaluation

It is important whenever you have completed a project to assess your work and think about how you might improve it. Review your investigation needs, activities, *Inquiry Journal* entries, and presentation for this unit. Then answer the following questions.

- Do you think you successfully achieved the purpose of your investigation? Why?

  Answers will vary.

  _____

- Do you think the details, facts, and supporting evidence you derived from your investigation were well represented in your presentation? Why?

  Answers will vary.

  _____

- How did you apply what you learned about conducting an investigation in Unit 1 to your Unit 2 investigation?

  Answers will vary.

  _____

- What about this investigation went particularly well?

  Answers will vary.

  _____

- How might you conduct your next investigation differently?

  Answers will vary.

  _____

Name _____ Date _____

Unit Wrap-Up

- How did you feel about this unit?

  ☐ I enjoyed it very much.   ☐ I liked it.

  ☐ I liked some of it.   ☐ I didn't like it.

- How would you rate the difficulty of this unit?

  ☐ easy   ☐ medium   ☐ hard

- How would you rate your performance during this unit?

  ☐ I learned a lot about astronomy.

  ☐ I learned some new things about astronomy.

  ☐ I didn't learn much about astronomy.

- Why did you choose this rating?

  Answers will vary.
  _____

  _____

- What was the most interesting thing you learned about astronomy?

  Answers will vary.
  _____

  _____

- Is there anything else about astronomy that you would like to learn? What?

  Answers will vary.
  _____

  _____

  _____

- What did you learn about astronomy that you didn't know before?

  Answers will vary.
  _____
  _____
  _____
  _____

- What did you learn about yourself as a learner?

  Answers will vary.
  _____
  _____
  _____
  _____

- What do you need to work on as a learner?

  Answers will vary.
  _____
  _____
  _____
  _____

- What resources (books, films, magazines, interviews, other) did you use on your own during this unit? Which of these were the most helpful? Why?

  Answers will vary.
  _____
  _____
  _____
  _____

UNIT 3 Heritage

Knowledge about Heritage

- This is what I know about heritage before reading the unit.

  Answers will vary.

  _____

  _____

  _____

  _____

  _____

  _____

- These are some things I would like to know about heritage.

  Answers will vary.

  _____

  _____

  _____

  _____

  _____

  _____

Reminder: I should read this page again when I get to the end of the unit to see how much I've learned about heritage.

Recording Concept Information

As I read each selection, I learned these new things about heritage.

- "The Land I Lost: Adventures of a Boy in Vietnam" by Huynh Quang Nhuong

  Answers will vary.
  _____
  _____
  _____
  _____

- "In Two Worlds: A Yup'ik Eskimo Family" by Aylette Jenness and Alice Rivers

  Answers will vary.
  _____
  _____
  _____
  _____

- "The West Side" by Peggy Mann

  Answers will vary.
  _____
  _____
  _____
  _____

- "Love As Strong As Ginger" by Lenore Look
  Answers will vary.

- "The Night Journey" by Kathryn Lasky
  Answers will vary.

- "Parmele" by Eloise Greenfield and Lessie Jones Little
  Answers will vary.

Conducting an Interview

Think about questions that you might ask the person you will interview. What do you especially want to know? How will talking to this person help you learn more about your heritage? Write some questions that will help you find out what you want to know. Discuss these questions with your classmates.

Questions about where my ancestors were born:

Answers will vary.

_____

_____

_____

_____

Questions about languages that my ancestors spoke:

Answers will vary.

_____

_____

_____

_____

Questions about traditions that have been passed down in my family or culture:

Answers will vary.

_____

_____

_____

_____

Conducting an Interview *(continued)*

Now organize the information you got from your interview.

Information about where my ancestors were born:

Answers will vary.

_____

_____

_____

Information about languages that my ancestors spoke:

Answers will vary.

_____

_____

_____

Information about traditions that have been passed down in my family or culture:

Answers will vary.

_____

_____

_____

Other information I learned:

Answers will vary.

_____

_____

_____

Ideas about Heritage

Of the ideas discussed in class about heritage, these are the ones I found most interesting. **Answers will vary.**

_____

_____

_____

_____

_____

_____

_____

_____

_____

_____

_____

_____

_____

_____

_____

_____

_____

_____

UNIT 3 Heritage

Comparison Chart

You have read about different Arctic peoples: the Tunrit, the Netsilik, Yup'iks of ancient and recent times, and Yup'iks of today. Think about how these peoples are similar and how they are different. Then fill in some of the spaces on the chart below.

Answers will vary.

	Tunrit	Netsilik	Yup'iks of Long Ago
Homes			
Food			
Clothing			
Transportation			
Education			
Community Life			

Yup'iks of 50 Years Ago	Yup'iks of 25 Years Ago	Yup'iks of Today

Identifying an Investigation Topic

Use the Idea Web below to help you identify an investigation topic that interests you. Begin by writing in the circle a word, phrase, or question that relates to the theme of heritage. On the lines that radiate from the circle, write other words or phrases that relate to what you wrote in the circle. Remember: No idea is a bad idea! **Answers will vary.**

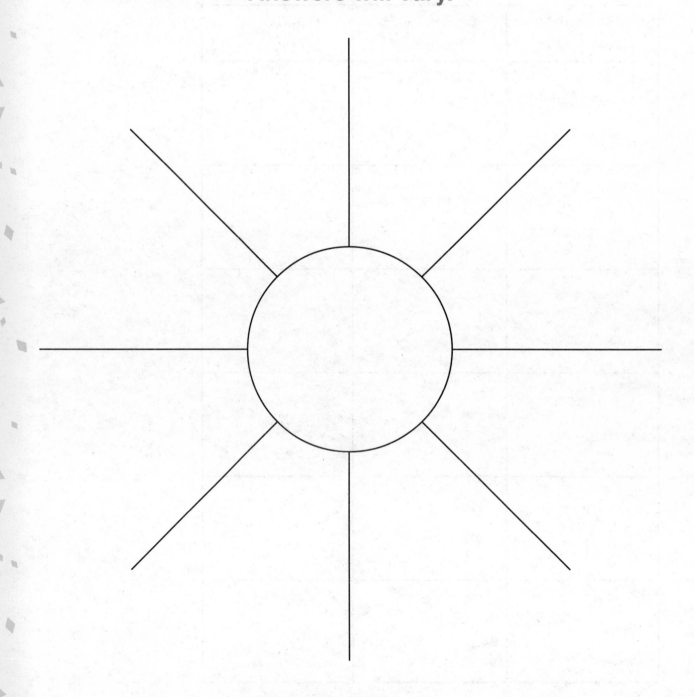

Formulating Questions and Problems

A good question or problem to investigate:
Answers will vary.

_____

_____

_____

_____

_____

Why this is an interesting question or problem:
Answers will vary.

_____

_____

_____

_____

_____

Some other things I wonder about this question or problem:
Answers will vary.

_____

_____

_____

_____

_____

Formulating Questions and Problems *(continued)*

My investigation group's question or problem:
Answers will vary.

_____

_____

_____

_____

_____

What our investigation will contribute to the rest of the class:
Answers will vary.

_____

_____

_____

_____

_____

Some other things I wonder about this question or problem:
Answers will vary.

_____

_____

_____

_____

_____

Using Time Lines

Using time lines allows one to summarize and organize events in the order in which they occurred. On the lines below, brainstorm some major events that occurred within your own family or circle of friends. For example, you might list birth dates, exciting trips you have taken, or a family move. Then, on the following page, create a time line of the events.

Answers will vary.

_____

_____

_____

_____

_____

_____

_____

_____

_____

_____

_____

_____

Title: _____

Making Conjectures

Our question or problem:
Answers will vary.
_____

_____

_____

_____

_____

Conjecture (my first theory or explanation):
Answers will vary.
_____

_____

_____

_____

_____

_____

_____

_____

   As you collect information, your conjecture will change.
Return to this page to record your new theories or
explanations about your question or problem.

Using Graphs

You can use a graph to show text information in a different way. Complete the graph below to make it illustrate the following quote from "The West Side."

"But the idea is, if you hit the ball past the first sewer, that's pretty good. If you hit it past the second sewer, that's sensational. And if you hit it past the third sewer, that's impossible. The third sewer's right down at the end of the street. You can hardly even see it from here."

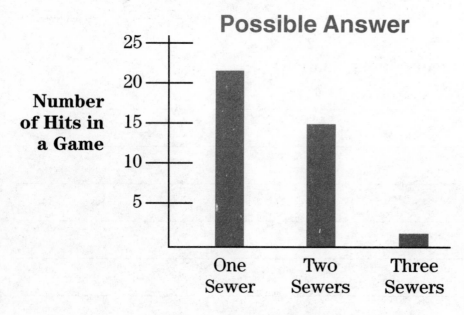

Possible Answer

Number of Hits in a Game

Distance Ball Was Hit

Use an encyclopedia, math book, or the Internet to find out more about different kinds of graphs, including line graphs and bar graphs. Then, use the space below to create a graph that shows something about your heritage. If possible, make a graph that illustrates your unit investigation findings.

Answers will vary.

UNIT 3 Heritage

Project Planning

Use the calendar to help schedule your heritage unit
investigation. Fill in the dates. Make sure that you mark any
days you know you will not be able to work. Then choose the
date on which you will start and the date on which you hope to

Sunday	Monday	Tuesday	Wednesday

finish. You may also find it helpful to mark the dates by which you hope to complete different parts of the investigation. Record what you accomplish each day.   **Answers will vary.**

Thursday	Friday	Saturday

UNIT 3 Heritage

Establishing Investigation Needs

My group's question or problem:
Answers will vary.

_____

_____

_____

_____

Knowledge Needs—Information I need to find or figure out
in order to investigate the question or problem: **Answers will vary.**

A. _____

B. _____

C. _____

D. _____

E. _____

Source	Useful?	How?
Encyclopedias		
Books		
Magazines		
Letters		
Videotapes, filmstrips, and so on		
Television		
Interviews, observations		
Museums		
Other:		

Drawing Conclusions from Multiple Sources

Think about and note how information from each of the resources listed below could add to your understanding of a person.

Possible answers are shown.

Resource	What I Could Learn About the Person I Interviewed
Map of area where the person grew up	Whether the person had a rural or urban hometown and the kinds of resources he or she was used to having available
Report cards from school(s)	Whether the person attended school regularly and what subjects might have been of most interest to him or her
Telephone book from city where the person lives	Approximate size of the town's population and whether this person might have relatives there with the same last name
Photo albums	How the person celebrated special occasions, the size of his or her family, and the events he or she wanted to record
Other: _____	Answers will vary.

Name _____ Date _____

Investigating a Variety of Cultures

You have read about families who live in very different places and who have very different heritages. Think about some of the different homes people live in, the different foods they eat, and the different ways they earn money. Then fill in

Selection	Setting	Homes

some of the spaces on the lines below. Continue to add information to these pages as you read other selections in the unit.

Answers will vary.

Foods	Ways People Earn Money	Other Differences

Name _____ Date _____

Establishing Investigation Plans

Our question or problem:

Answers will vary. _____

_____

_____

_____

_____

Knowledge Needs—Information we need to find or figure
out in order to investigate the question or problem:

A. **Answers will vary.** _____

B. _____

C. _____

D. _____

E. _____

F. _____

Group Members	Main Jobs

Hint: To save rewriting Knowledge Needs in the
Main Jobs section, put in the capital letter marking
the Knowledge Needs line.

Name _____ Date _____

Using Technology in Investigations

Use technology to find out more about people who have immigrated to the United States. Then share your findings with the class.

- I want to focus on this aspect of immigration:
  Answers will vary.
  _____

- These are resources I will use to get statistics:
  Possible answers include the Internet, a library
  computer catalog, and microfilm and microfiche.
  _____

- These are interesting statistics I found:
  Answers will vary.
  _____
  _____
  _____
  _____
  _____
  _____
  _____

Name _____ Date _____

Multimedia Presentations

Audiovisual resources can add meaning and enjoyment to a presentation. Consider what you could do to add a special touch to the presentation of your investigation findings.

- What song or type of music will go with your presentation?
  Answers will vary.
  _____

  _____

  _____

- What type of artwork would best express the feeling or meaning of your story?
  Answers will vary.
  _____

  _____

  _____

  _____

- What video could you create to enhance your presentation?
  Answers will vary.
  _____

  _____

  _____

  _____

Name _____ Date _____

Unit Wrap-Up

- How did you feel about this unit?

  ☐ I enjoyed it very much.   ☐ I liked it.

  ☐ I liked some of it.   ☐ I didn't like it.

- How would you rate the difficulty of this unit?

  ☐ easy   ☐ medium   ☐ hard

- How would you rate your performance during this unit?

  ☐ I learned a lot about heritage.

  ☐ I learned some new things about heritage.

  ☐ I didn't learn much about heritage.

- Why did you choose this rating?

  Answers will vary.
  _____

  _____

- What was the most interesting thing you learned
  about heritage?

  Answers will vary.
  _____

  _____

- Is there anything else about heritage that you would
  like to learn? What?

  Answers will vary.
  _____

  _____

  _____

- What did you learn about heritage that you didn't know before?

  Answers will vary.

  _____

  _____

  _____

- What did you learn about yourself as a learner?

  Answers will vary.

  _____

  _____

  _____

- What do you need to work on as a learner?

  Answers will vary.

  _____

  _____

  _____

- What resources (books, films, magazines, interviews, other) did you use on your own during this unit? Which of these were the most helpful? Why?

  Answers will vary.

  _____

  _____

  _____

  _____

Name _____ Date _____

Knowledge about Making a New Nation

- This is what I know about the American Revolution time period before reading this unit.

Answers will vary.

_____

_____

_____

_____

_____

- These are some things I would like to know about the American Revolution time period.

Answers will vary.

_____

_____

_____

_____

_____

Reminder: I should read this page again when I get to the end of the unit to see how much I've learned about the American Revolution.

UNIT 4 Making a New Nation

Recording Concept Information

As I read each selection, I learned these new things about making a new nation.

- "If You Lived at the Time of the American Revolution"
  by Kay Moore
  Answers will vary.

  _____

  _____

  _____

  _____

- "The Night the Revolution Began" by Russell Freedman
  Answers will vary.

  _____

  _____

  _____

  _____

- "The Midnight Ride of Paul Revere"
  by Henry Wadsworth Longfellow
  Answers will vary.

  _____

  _____

  _____

  _____

- "The Declaration of Independence" by R. Conrad Stein

Answers will vary.

_____

_____

_____

_____

_____

_____

_____

- "The Master Spy of Yorktown" by Burke Davis

Answers will vary.

_____

_____

_____

_____

_____

_____

_____

_____

- "Shh! We're Writing the Constitution" by Jean Fritz
  Answers will vary.

- "We, the People of the United States" by Milton Meltzer
  Answers will vary.

About the American Revolution

- These are some things I learned about an event or person from the American Revolution time period:

Answers will vary.

_____

_____

_____

_____

_____

_____

_____

- This is how that event or person influenced the outcome of the American Revolution.

Answers will vary.

_____

_____

_____

_____

_____

_____

_____

About the American Revolution *(continued)*

- These are some ways in which the United States was affected by that event or person:

  Answers will vary.

  _____

  _____

  _____

  _____

  _____

  _____

  _____

- This is how that event or person influenced my life in the United States of America:

  Answers will vary.

  _____

  _____

  _____

  _____

  _____

  _____

  _____

Name _____ Date _____

Ideas about Making a New Nation

Of the ideas discussed in class about Making a New Nation, these are the ones I found most interesting.

Answers will vary.

_____

_____

_____

_____

_____

_____

_____

_____

_____

_____

_____

_____

_____

_____

_____

_____

_____

UNIT 4 Making a New Nation

Analyzing Media Sources

Write examples on the lines provided of how the short film you watched:

Entertained: _____ Answers will vary. _____

_____

_____

_____

Informed: _____ Answers will vary. _____

_____

_____

_____

Persuaded: _____ Answers will vary. _____

_____

_____

_____

Interpreted events: _____ Answers will vary. _____

_____

_____

_____

Transmitted culture: _____ Answers will vary. _____

_____

_____

_____

Name _____ Date _____

Formulating Questions and Problems

- A good question or problem to investigate:
Answers will vary.

_____

_____

_____

_____

_____

- Why this is an interesting question or problem:
Answers will vary.

_____

_____

_____

_____

_____

- Some other things I wonder about this question or problem:
Answers will vary.

_____

_____

_____

_____

_____

Formulating Questions and Problems *(continued)*

- My investigation group's question or problem:

Answers will vary.

_____

_____

_____

_____

- What our investigation will contribute to the rest of
  the class:

Answers will vary.

_____

_____

_____

_____

- Some other things I wonder about this question or problem:

Answers will vary.

_____

_____

_____

_____

Name _____ Date _____

Using a CD-ROM Encyclopedia

Write directions for how to use a CD-ROM encyclopedia using Help instructions found on your computer and on the CD-ROM.

How to open the CD-ROM on a computer: _**Answers will vary.**_

_____

_____

How to search for information: _**Answers will vary.**_

_____

_____

Now answer the following questions by conducting a CD-ROM encyclopedia search.

What is my investigation topic? _**Answers will vary.**_

What is the name of the CD-ROM I am using? _**Answers will**_

_____

What information did I find on my investigation topic? _____
**Answers will vary.**

_____

_____

_____

_____

_____

Name _____ Date _____

Making Conjectures

Our question or problem:
Answers will vary.

_____

_____

_____

_____

_____

Conjecture (my first theory or explanation):
Answers will vary.

_____

_____

_____

_____

_____

_____

_____

As you collect information, your conjecture will change. Return to this page to record your new theories or explanations about your question or problem.

Name _____ Date _____

Using a Map

The United States in the 1780s

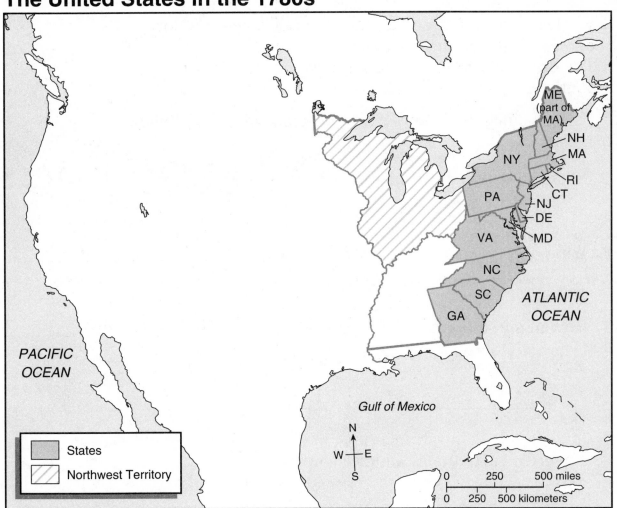

Maps are drawings that show where places or landmarks are located and that have certain features. These include a title, a key, a scale, and a compass rose. Some maps show important and interesting information about the past.

Using a Map *(continued)*

Maps have the following features:
- The **title** tells what information the map shows or what the map's purpose is. For instance, the map on page 97 shows the United States as it was in the 1780s.
- The **key** tells what each special symbol or color on the map stands for.
- The **scale** shows how many miles or kilometers are represented by a given measure, usually some fraction of an inch or centimeter.
- The **direction arrows** or **compass rose** shows north, south, east, and west on the map.

Using the map on the previous page, answer the following questions.

1. What is the title of the map? __The United States in the 1780s__

2. What does the map key show? __It shows how to tell the__ __states from the Northwest Territory.__

3. How many states are shown on the map? __Thirteen__ __(In the 1780s, Maine was part of Massachusetts).__

4. If you are in Pennsylvania (PA), in what direction would you go to get to the Atlantic Ocean?
   __East__

5. About how many miles is it from the westernmost edge of the Northwest Territory to the Pacific Ocean?
   __About 1350 miles__

How might you use a map in your investigation?

Name _____ Date _____

Establishing Investigation Needs

My group's question or problem:
Answers will vary.

_____

_____

_____

_____

Knowledge Needs—Information I need to find or figure out
in order to investigate the question or problem:

A. Answers will vary. _____

B. _____

C. _____

D. _____

E. _____

Source	Useful?	How?
Encyclopedias		
Books		
Magazines		
Letters on Volumes		
Videotapes, filmstrips, and so on		
Television		
Interviews, observations		
Museums		
Other:		

Name _____ Date _____

Project Planning

Use the calendar to help schedule your unit investigation of Making a New Nation. Fill in the dates. Make sure that you mark any days you know you will not be able to work. Then choose the date on which you will start and the date on which

Sunday	Monday	Tuesday	Wednesday

you hope to finish. You may also find it helpful to mark the dates by which you hope to complete different parts of the investigation. Record what you accomplish each day.

Answers will vary.

Thursday	Friday	Saturday

UNIT 4 Making a New Nation

Effects of the American Revolution

The lives of many people were changed by the American Revolution. On the charts on these two pages, list the resources you have used to investigate the effects of the war

Answers will vary.

Resource	People (Characters)	How They Were Affected

on people's lives. Then tell who was affected and how they were affected. Discuss your charts and your ideas with your classmates.

Resource	People (Characters)	How They Were Affected

Name _____ Date _____

Establishing Investigation Plans

Our question or problem:
Answers will vary.

_____

_____

_____

_____

Knowledge Needs—Information we need to find or figure
out in order to investigate the question or problem:

A. **Answers will vary.** _____

B. _____

C. _____

D. _____

E. _____

F. _____

Group Members	Main Jobs

Hint: To save rewriting Knowledge Needs in the
Main Jobs section, put in the capital letter marking
the Knowledge Needs line.

Paraphrasing

Paraphrasing is writing the main ideas of a source in your own words. Sometimes it is useful to include in your paraphrase a direct quote, or exact wording used in the original source. When doing this, be sure to put the direct quote within quotation marks. Then write in parentheses the name of the source from which the quoted material came.

The following is a firsthand account of the British surrender at Yorktown. It is from the journal of James Thatcher, an army doctor who witnessed it. Read the paragraph, then paraphrase it on the lines provided. In your paraphrase, include at least one direct quote. (If necessary, use a dictionary to clarify unfamiliar words.)

> **"It was about two o'clock when the captive army advanced through the line formed from their reception. Every eye was prepared to gaze on Lord Cornwallis, the object of particular interest and solicitude, but he disappointed our anxious expectations. Pretending indisposition, he made General O'Hara his substitute as the leader of the army. The officer was followed by the conquered troops in a slow and solemn step, with shouldered arms, colors cased, and drums beating a British march. . . ."**

—*A Military Journal*, Thatcher, 1827.

Answers will vary.

_____

_____

_____

_____

_____

UNIT 4 Making a New Nation

Primary Sources

Think about things you have read that are primary sources.
Then record examples on the lines below.
Answers will vary.

Title: _____ Author: _____

Type of primary source: _____

What did you learn from this? _____

_____

_____

Title: _____ Author: _____

Type of primary source: _____

What did you learn from this? _____

_____

_____

Title: _____ Author: _____

Type of primary source: _____

What did you learn from this? _____

_____

_____

Name _____ Date _____

Feedback

If you gave an informal presentation of your investigation findings, record notes on the feedback you received on the lines provided. Reference these notes as you make decisions about how to revise your presentation.

Answers will vary.

_____

_____

_____

_____

_____

_____

_____

_____

_____

_____

_____

_____

_____

_____

_____

_____

Using Technology in Presentations

On the lines provided, write ideas about how each of the technological devices below might be used to enhance the presentation of your investigation findings.

Videotape player: **Answers will vary.** _____

_____

Tape recorder: _____

_____

The Internet: _____

_____

Slide projector: _____

_____

Overhead projector: _____

_____

Word processing or illustration program: _____

_____

Now, choose the device from above that you think will best enhance your presentation. On the line below, write the name of the person you will need to contact for permission to use the device and instruction on how it works.

_____

Name _____ Date _____

Persuasion in Advertisements

Use the lines below to record notes from your discussion about television advertisements.

Some persuasive techniques used in advertisements are:

Answers will vary. Students may mention

techniques such as supporting viewpoints with

facts, using flattery or exaggeration, or making

List some spoken messages used in the advertisements:

Answers will vary. Students should cite things that

speakers told the audience to do, such as buy

something, go somewhere, or support a cause.

List some unspoken messages from the advertisements.
(These may be expressed through visual elements or inferred
from something the speaker says or does.):

Answers will vary. Students may mention that

speakers were portrayed as being especially fun

loving, wise, intelligent, or well liked so that

audience members would want to be like them.

Now, list some ways you might use some of the techniques
you wrote about above in the advertisement you are creating
for your investigation activity.

_____

_____

_____

UNIT 4 Making a New Nation

Unit Wrap-Up

- How did you feel about this unit?

  ☐ I enjoyed it very much.   ☐ I liked it.

  ☐ I liked some of it.   ☐ I didn't like it.

- How would you rate the difficulty of this unit?

  ☐ easy   ☐ medium   ☐ hard

- How would you rate your performance during this unit?

  ☐ I learned a lot about making a new nation.

  ☐ I learned some new things about making a new nation.

  ☐ I didn't learn much about making a new nation.

- Why did you choose this rating?

  Answers will vary.

  _____

  _____

- What was the most interesting thing you learned about making a new nation?

  Answers will vary.

  _____

  _____

- Is there anything else about making a new nation that you would like to learn? What?

  Answers will vary.

  _____

  _____

- What did you learn about making a new nation that you didn't know before?

  Answers will vary.

  _____

  _____

  _____

- What did you learn about yourself as a learner?

  Answers will vary.

  _____

  _____

  _____

- What do you need to work on as a learner?

  Answers will vary.

  _____

  _____

  _____

- What resources (books, films, magazines, interviews, other) did you use on your own during this unit? Which of these were the most helpful? Why?

  Answers will vary.

  _____

  _____

  _____

UNIT 5 Going West

Knowledge about Going West

- This is what I know about the American West before reading the unit.

  Answers will vary.

  _____

  _____

  _____

  _____

  _____

  _____

- These are some things I would like to know about the American West.

  Answers will vary.

  _____

  _____

  _____

  _____

  _____

Reminder: I should read this page again when I get to the end of the unit to see how much I've learned about Going West.

Name _____ Date _____

Recording Concept Information

As I read each selection, I learned these new things about the American West.

- "Sacagawea's Journey" by Betty Westrom Skold
  Answers will vary.

  _____

  _____

  _____

  _____

- "Buffalo Hunt" by Russell Freedman
  Answers will vary.

  _____

  _____

  _____

  _____

- "The Journal of Wong Ming-Chung" by Laurence Yep
  Answers will vary.

  _____

  _____

  _____

  _____

Recording Concept Information *(continued)*

- "The Coming of the Long Knives" by Scott O'Dell

  Answers will vary.

  _____

  _____

  _____

  _____

  _____

  _____

  _____

  _____

  _____

- "Old Yeller and the Bear" by Fred Gipson

  Answers will vary.

  _____

  _____

  _____

  _____

  _____

  _____

  _____

  _____

  _____

- "Bill Pickett: Rodeo-Ridin' Cowboy" by Andrea D. Pinkney

Answers will vary.

_____

_____

_____

_____

_____

_____

_____

_____

- "McBroom the Rainmaker" by Sid Fleischman

Answers will vary.

_____

_____

_____

_____

_____

_____

_____

_____

UNIT 5 Going West

Changes in the American West

Many changes occurred as the American West was being settled. Throughout your reading and investigation for this unit, record these changes on the chart. For each change, list the causes, the groups involved, and the effects on the people of the region. **Answers will vary.**

Change	Causes

Groups Involved	Effects

UNIT 5 Going West

The Geography of the American West

Throughout your reading and investigation for this unit, record the different landforms found in the American West. To illustrate each type, draw a picture or cut out a photo from a magazine or a travel brochure.

Landform	Characteristics	Location
mesa	steep walls flat top dry	Southwest U.S. (Arizona, New Mexico)

Beside each picture, list the characteristics of the landform and the states in which it can be found. Maps and atlases will be helpful resources. **Answers will vary.**

Landform	Characteristics	Location

Name _____ Date _____

Ideas about Going West

Of the ideas discussed in class about the American West, these are the ones I found most interesting.

Answers will vary.

_____

_____

_____

_____

_____

_____

_____

_____

_____

_____

_____

_____

_____

_____

_____

_____

_____

_____

_____

Telling Stories with Maps

Based on what you have read in the selection "Sacagawea's Journey," draw a map that shows the westward route taken by the Lewis and Clark expedition.

In your map, remember to include a compass rose, a key, and labels for important locations and physical features, such as mountains and rivers. Use captions to describe what happened at important points along the journey. Refer to an atlas to help you draw your map.

Maps will vary.

Name _____ Date _____

Formulating Questions and Problems

A good question or problem to investigate:

Answers will vary.

_____

_____

_____

_____

Why this is an interesting question or problem:

Answers will vary.

_____

_____

_____

_____

Some other things I wonder about this question or problem:

Answers will vary.

_____

_____

_____

_____

My investigation group's question or problem:

Answers will vary.

_____

_____

_____

_____

_____

What our investigation will contribute to the rest of the class:

Answers will vary.

_____

_____

_____

_____

_____

Some other things I wonder about this question or problem:

Answers will vary.

_____

_____

_____

_____

_____

Audio Resources

Below list the five types of audio resources that you like listening to the most. Then beside each write what kind of information each type might offer for your investigation.

Audio Resource 1: ___ **Answers will vary.** _____

Information offered: _____

_____

Audio Resource 2: _____

Information offered: _____

_____

Audio Resource 3: _____

Information offered: _____

_____

Audio Resource 4: _____

Information offered: _____

_____

Audio Resource 5: _____

Information offered: _____

_____

From the list you created, choose the audio resource that you think is most likely to provide information valuable to your investigation. On the following lines, write places you might find this type of resource. Then write three questions you would like to answer using this resource.

Audio Resource: ____**Answers will vary.**_____ _____

Where I might find it:

- _____ _____

- _____ _____

- _____

What I want to learn:

Question 1: _____

_____

_____

_____

Question 2: _____

_____

_____

_____

Question 3: _____

_____

_____

_____

UNIT 5 Going West

Making Conjectures

Our question or problem:

Answers will vary.
_____
_____
_____
_____
_____

Conjecture (my first theory or explanation):

Answers will vary.
_____
_____
_____
_____
_____
_____
_____
_____

   As you collect information, your conjecture will change.
Return to this page to record your new theories or
explanations about your question or problem.

Name _____ Date _____

Establishing Investigation Needs

My group's question or problem:
Answers will vary.

_____

_____

_____

_____

Knowledge Needs—Information I need to find or figure out
in order to investigate the question or problem:

A. **Answers will vary.** _____

B. _____

C. _____

D. _____

E. _____

Source	Useful?	How?
Encyclopedias		
Books		
Magazines		
Letters on Volumes		
Videotapes, filmstrips, and so on		
Television		
Interviews, observations		
Museums		
Other:		

Name _____ Date _____

Project Planning

Use the calendar to help schedule your unit investigation of the American West. Fill in the dates. Make sure that you mark any days you know you will not be able to work. Then choose the date on which you will start and the date on which you

Sunday	Monday	Tuesday	Wednesday

Project Planning • Inquiry Journal

hope to finish. You may also find it helpful to mark the dates
by which you hope to complete different parts of the
investigation. Record what you accomplish each day.

Answers will vary.

Thursday	Friday	Saturday

UNIT 5 Going West

Verifying Facts and Comparing Sources

List four facts from "The Coming of the Long Knives." List the sources you might use to verify each fact.

Atlas: a book containing many maps
Almanac: a book containing up-to-date facts, published each year
Encyclopedia: a book or set of books with information on many topics, arranged in alphabetical order
Biographical dictionary: a dictionary containing facts about famous people
Geographical dictionary: a dictionary containing facts about places

---

Fact: **Answers will vary.** _____

_____

Sources: _____

Fact: _____

_____

Sources: _____

Fact: _____

_____

Sources: _____

Fact: _____

_____

Sources: _____

Choose two sources that you are using for your investigation. Complete this page to evaluate the sources and the information they provide.

Answers will vary.

Source: _____

Date of publication: _____

Author's experience/qualifications: _____

_____

Does the author's bias influence the way facts are presented?

_____

Is detailed information provided? _____

How would you rate the usefulness of this source?

_____

_____

Source: _____

Date of publication: _____

Author's experience/qualifications: _____

_____

Does the author's bias influence the way facts are presented?

_____

Is detailed information provided? _____

How would you rate the usefulness of this source?

_____

_____

Name _____ Date _____

Problems in the American West

Life in the American West was full of challenges. The people of the region faced many dangers, conflicts, and other difficulties. Throughout your reading and investigation for the unit, list some problems the people of the American West faced. Write a brief description of how they handled or solved each problem.   **Answers will vary.**

Problem	**Solutions**
_____	_____
_____	_____
_____	_____
_____	_____
_____	_____

Problem	**Solutions**
_____	_____
_____	_____
_____	_____
_____	_____

Problem   **Solutions**

_____	▶	_____

Problem   **Solutions**

_____	▶	_____

Problem   **Solutions**

_____	▶	_____

Name _____ Date _____

Establishing Investigation Plans

Our question or problem:
Answers will vary.

_____

_____

_____

_____

_____

Knowledge Needs—Information we need to find or figure
out in order to investigate the question or problem:

A. **Answers will vary.** _____

B. _____

C. _____

D. _____

E. _____

F. _____

Group Members	Main Jobs

Hint: To save rewriting Knowledge Needs in the
Main Jobs section, put in the capital letter marking
the Knowledge Needs line.

Feedback

If you gave an informal presentation of your investigation findings, record notes on the feedback you received on the lines provided. Reference these notes as you make decisions about how to revise your presentation.

Answers will vary.

_____

_____

_____

_____

_____

_____

_____

_____

_____

_____

_____

_____

_____

_____

_____

_____

Using Technology

Write instructions for completing the following operations on your word processing program. If needed, use the Help function to assist you in writing the instructions. Note that the directions for completing a function may differ from one word processing program to another. **Answers will vary.**

Example: **Make a word boldface: Highlight the word and click the Boldface button on the menu bar.**

Operation	Instructions
Create a new document.	
Save a new document.	
Print a document.	
Delete a piece of text.	
Move a piece of text.	
Find and replace misspelled words.	
Find a word's synonym.	
Create a table.	
Insert clipart.	
Make a bulleted list.	

Name _____ Date _____

Interpreting Graphs

Study the following graph. Then, use information in the graph and what you have learned from the stories and activities in this unit to answer the questions.

**Population Growth in Selected
Western States, 1860–1900**

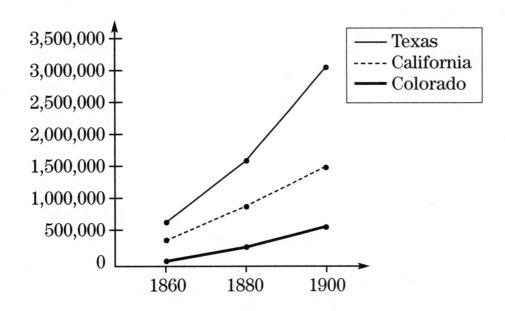

- Which state probably had the most opportunities for making a living between 1860 and 1900? Explain your answer.

  Texas. This state had the greatest increase in

  population. The cattle industry attracted many

  people to Texas.

- Many families lived on farms in the 1800s. Which state may not have been good for farming? Explain.

  Colorado. This state had the smallest population

  growth. Mountainous land may have made

  farming difficult.

Read the following paragraph. Then, use the information to make a line graph titled "Population Growth in Dallas."

Dallas, Texas, is currently one of the largest cities in the United States, but it was not always so big. In fact, in the 1850s it had only a few stores and saddle shops. However, because it was a convenient place for people on nearby farms and ranches to buy their supplies, it began to grow. In 1860, Dallas had a population of 678, and a hotel, a sawmill, and a flour mill were opened. After the Civil War, many freed slaves came to Dallas to work, and the population grew to 3,000 in 1870. With the coming of the railroad in the early 1870s, Dallas's economy began to boom. Dallas was the world center of the buffalo-hide trade. More and more merchants set up shop in Dallas, and by 1880 the population had grown to 10,385.

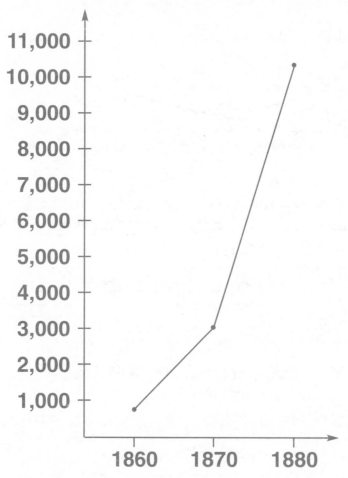

Population Growth in Dallas

Unit Wrap-Up

- How did you feel about this unit?

  ☐ I enjoyed it very much.   ☐ I liked it.

  ☐ I liked some of it.   ☐ I didn't like it.

- How would you rate the difficulty of this unit?

  ☐ easy   ☐ medium   ☐ hard

- How would you rate your performance during this unit?

  ☐ I learned a lot about the American West.

  ☐ I learned some new things about the American West.

  ☐ I didn't learn much about the American West.

- Why did you choose this rating?

  Answers will vary.

  _____

- What was the most interesting thing you learned about the American West?

  Answers will vary.

  _____

- Is there anything else about the American West that you would like to learn? What?

  Answers will vary.

  _____

Unit Wrap-Up *(continued)*

- What did you learn about the American West that you didn't
  know before?

  Answers will vary.

- What did you learn about yourself as a learner?

  Answers will vary.

- What do you need to work on as a learner?

  Answers will vary.

- What resources (books, films, magazines, interviews, other)
  did you use on your own during this unit? Which of these
  were the most helpful? Why?

  Answers will vary.

Knowledge about Journeys and Quests

- This is what I know about journeys and quests before reading the unit.

  Answers will vary.
  _____

  _____

  _____

  _____

  _____

  _____

- These are some things I would like to know about journeys and quests.

  Answers will vary.
  _____

  _____

  _____

  _____

  _____

  _____

Reminder: I should read this page again when I get to the end of the unit to see how much I've learned about journeys and quests.

Name _____ Date _____

Recording Concept Information

As I read each selection, I learned these new things about journeys and quests.

- "The Story of Jumping Mouse" by John Steptoe
  Answers will vary.
  _____
  _____
  _____
  _____

- "Trapped by the Ice!" by Michael McCurdy
  Answers will vary.
  _____
  _____
  _____
  _____

- "Apollo *11*: First Moon Landing" by Michael D. Cole
  Answers will vary.
  _____
  _____
  _____
  _____

- "When Shlemiel Went to Warsaw" by Isaac Bashevis Singer
  Answers will vary.

  _____

  _____

  _____

  _____

  _____

- "The Search" by Joseph Krumgold
  Answers will vary.

  _____

  _____

  _____

  _____

  _____

- "Alberic the Wise" by Norton Juster
  Answers will vary.

  _____

  _____

  _____

  _____

  _____

UNIT 6 Journeys and Quests

Ideas about Journeys and Quests

Of the ideas discussed in class about journeys and quests, these are the ones I found most interesting.

Answers will vary.

_____

_____

_____

_____

_____

_____

_____

_____

_____

_____

_____

_____

_____

_____

_____

_____

_____

_____

_____

_____

Risk and Motivation

Often there are dangers or sacrifices involved in taking a journey. People who decide to pursue a dangerous quest are usually motivated by powerful reasons. Briefly list the dangers Sir Ernest Shackleton and his crew faced as well as their motivations. Then think about the motivations of other journeyers you read about and about the risks or hardships involved in their journeys. **Answers will vary.**

Journeyer	Motivation	Dangers Faced/ Hardships Endured

UNIT 6 Journeys and Quests

Formulating Questions and Problems

A good question or problem to investigate:
Answers will vary.

_____

_____

_____

_____

_____

Why this is an interesting question or problem:
Answers will vary.

_____

_____

_____

_____

_____

Some other things I wonder about this question or problem:
Answers will vary.

_____

_____

_____

_____

_____

My investigation group's question or problem:

Answers will vary.

_____

_____

_____

_____

_____

What our investigation will contribute to the rest of the class:

Answers will vary.

_____

_____

_____

_____

_____

Some other things I wonder about this question or problem:

Answers will vary.

_____

_____

_____

_____

_____

UNIT 6 Journeys and Quests

Making Conjectures

Our question or problem:

Answers will vary.

_____

_____

_____

_____

_____

Conjecture (my first theory or explanation):

Answers will vary.

_____

_____

_____

_____

_____

_____

_____

_____

As you collect information, your conjecture will change.
Return to this page to record your new theories or
explanations about your question or problem.

Mapping Journeys

Draw a map of a journey, real or imaginary, that you would like to take. Be sure to include a map key, distance scale, and a compass rose (or direction arrows).

Maps will vary.

Write a caption for your map.

Captions will vary.

_____

_____

_____

_____

Name _____ Date _____

New Perspectives

Shlemiel left Chelm in order to find something new. Instead, he unwittingly found a new way to look at familiar people and things. Use the space below to record the new perspectives Shlemiel gained from his journey. Then record information about new perspectives or new ideas gained by other journeyers you have investigated. **Answers will vary.**

Journeyer	New Perspectives

New Perspectives • Inquiry Journal

Name _____ Date _____

Establishing Investigation Needs

My group's question or problem:
__Answers will vary.__
_____
_____
_____
_____

Knowledge Needs—Information I need to find or figure out
in order to investigate the question or problem:

A. __Answers will vary._____

B. _____

C. _____

D. _____

E. _____

Source	Useful?	How?
Atlases		
Books		
Magazines		
Newspapers		
Videotapes, filmstrips, and so on		
Television		
Interviews, observations		
Museums		
Other:		

Name _____ Date _____

Project Planning

Use the calendar to help schedule your journeys and quests unit investigation. Fill in the dates. Make sure that you mark any days you know you will not be able to work. Then choose the date on which you will start and the date on which you

Sunday	Monday	Tuesday	Wednesday

hope to finish. You may also find it helpful to mark the dates by which you hope to complete different parts of the investigation. Record what you accomplish each day.

Answers will vary.

Thursday	Friday	Saturday

Name _____ Date _____

Choosing Multiple Resources

When choosing resources for your investigation, it is important to keep in mind the usefulness of each resource. However, you should also feel free to choose resources that will be enjoyable to you as well as informative. Fill in the information requested below and keep it in mind when conducting resource searches. **Answers will vary.**

• Who are my favorite authors? _____

_____

• What writing styles do I like best (for example, formal,

informal, dialogue, and so on)? _____

_____

• What are themes that I find interesting? _____

_____

• What genres do I like the most? _____

_____

• What reading difficulty level am I most comfortable with? _____

_____

• What are some book titles on the theme of Journeys and

Quests that have been recommended to me? _____

_____

_____

Name _____ Date _____

Establishing Investigation Plans

Our question or problem:

Answers will vary.

_____

_____

_____

_____

_____

Knowledge Needs—Information we need to find or figure
out in order to investigate the question or problem:

Answers will vary.

A. _____

B. _____

C. _____

D. _____

E. _____

F. _____

Group Members	Main Jobs

Hint: To save rewriting Knowledge Needs in the
Main Jobs section, put in the capital letter marking
the Knowledge Needs line.

UNIT 6 Journeys and Quests

Structuring an Oral Presentation

Begin your presentation by telling what question or problem you investigated and stating your final revised conjecture.

Question or problem: _Answers will vary._____

Conjecture: _Answers will vary._____

Create the body of your presentation, or its middle part, by telling what information supported or disproved your final revised conjecture. Answers will vary.

Information that supported my conjecture:

A: _____

B: _____

C: _____

Information that disproved my conjecture:

A: _____

B: _____

C: _____

End the presentation by telling what conclusions you have drawn from your investigation and what unanswered questions you still have. Answers will vary.

Conclusions: _____

_____

Unanswered questions: _____

_____

Getting at Meaning

For this unit, you have read many stories about the concepts *journeys* and *quests*. The following questions will help you find connections between the stories and what they say about the concepts. You can use these connections as support for your investigations.

Answers will vary.
Possible answers are shown.

Characters

• How were the characters' motives for journeys and quests similar?

They all expected to learn something from their

journeys.

_____

• What were some different motives that the characters had?

Some characters wanted to prove themselves, some

hoped to help others, and some wanted to do

something that was exciting.

Settings

• How were some settings from your reading similar?

Most of the stories were set in places that were

unfamiliar or exciting.

_____

- What is one way all of the settings differed from each other?

They were placed in different time periods.

_____

_____

Solutions and Problems

- What was similar about how characters solved their problems?

All of the characters solved their problems by

adapting to an unforeseen condition.

_____

- What are two similar problems that had different solutions?

Shlemiel and Alberic both ended up in the wrong

place. Shlemiel solved this problem by staying and

Alberic solved it by leaving.

_____

Think about a personal experience you have had with journeys or quests. What were your motives for making the journey or quest? What was the setting for your experience? How did you solve the problems you encountered? Write a paragraph in which these questions are answered on the lines below.

_____

_____

_____

_____

_____

Unit Wrap-Up

- How did you feel about this unit?

  ☐ I enjoyed it very much.   ☐ I liked it.

  ☐ I liked some of it.   ☐ I didn't like it.

- How would you rate the difficulty of this unit?

  ☐ easy   ☐ medium   ☐ hard

- How would you rate your performance during this unit?

  ☐ I learned a lot about journeys and quests.

  ☐ I learned some new things about journeys and quests.

  ☐ I didn't learn much about journeys and quests.

- Why did you choose this rating?

  Answers will vary.
  _____

  _____

- What was the most interesting thing you learned about journeys and quests?

  Answers will vary.
  _____

  _____

- Is there anything else about journeys and quests that you would like to learn? What?

  Answers will vary.
  _____

  _____

- What did you learn about journeys and quests that you didn't know before?

  Answers will vary.

- What did you learn about yourself as a learner?

  Answers will vary.

- What do you need to work on as a learner?

  Answers will vary.

- What resources (books, films, magazines, interviews, other) did you use on your own during this unit? Which of these were the most helpful? Why?

  Answers will vary.